Changing Kids' Lives One Quote At a Time

121 Inspirational Sayings to Build Character in Children

By Steve Reifman

<u>Endorsements</u>

Dedication

To Mom, Dad, Lynn, Jeff, Sylvia, Alan, Ari, and Jordy

To all the family, friends, teachers, and students whose support, expertise, and encouragement made this book possible

About the Author

Steve Reifman is a National Board Certified elementary school teacher, writer, and speaker in Santa Monica, CA. Steve is the acclaimed author of several resource books for educators, including _Eight Essentials for Empowered Teaching and Learning, K-8_. He is also the creator of the Chase Manning Mystery Series for children 8-12 years of age. Each book in the series features a single-day, real-time thriller that occurs on an elementary school campus.

You can find weekly Teaching Tips, blog posts, and other valuable resources and strategies for teaching the whole child at _http://stevereifman.com_. You can follow Steve on Twitter at _http://twitter.com/#!/stevereifman_.

Introduction

Created for parents and teachers by a teacher, this book contains 121 inspirational quotes designed to bring out the best in children and develop lasting habits. For educators, discussing these quotes also helps establish an enthusiastic, productive, team-oriented classroom culture. Specifically, these quotes target 13 "Habits of Character," a list that includes Cooperation, Courage, Fairness, Honesty, Kindness, Patience, Perseverance, Positive Attitude, Pride, Respect, Responsibility, Self-discipline, and Service.

In addition, the quotes touch on other important ideas, such as quality, success, and health & wellness. From beginning to end, the quotes spiral through these topics to empower children with multiple opportunities to think about and discuss each one.

How Parents Can Use This Book

Make this book a regular part of your daily or weekly family routine. At least once a week, post a quote on a refrigerator or bulletin board, discuss it before school or at bedtime, or incorporate a conversation into family meals or car rides.

Whatever the venue, begin by having your child read the quote aloud. Next, provide your child with 30-60 seconds to think about the quote's meaning and relevance. Then, ask your child to share his or her thoughts with you. Together, you may choose to identify the habit or larger idea the quote addresses, offer interpretations of the quote's meaning, or share examples demonstrating how the quote applies to your daily lives. Emphasize that there are no right or wrong answers.

How Teachers Can Use This Book

In the classroom the book can function as a "Quote of the Day" calendar. Make this calendar a regular part of your morning routine. Two or three times a week, write a quote on the board and choose someone to read it aloud to the class. After providing students with time to think about the quote's meaning and relevance, do a pair-share to maximize participation in the activity. Then select a few volunteers to share their thoughts with the group.

In these whole class discussions students may choose to identify the habit or larger idea the quote addresses, offer interpretations of the quote's meaning, or share examples demonstrating how the quote applies to their daily lives. Emphasize that there are no right or wrong answers.

Benefits of Discussing These Quotes

Though the conversations take only a few minutes, the exercise is a valuable one because it encourages kids to think deeply, because there's a high tone to the dialogue that appeals to the best in people, and because it allows your family or classroom to start the day on a positive note.

Further payoffs to consistent use of this activity include better student behavior, stronger work habits and social skills, improved attitudes towards school, greater enthusiasm for and increased dedication to learning, more connections made between school and students' present and future lives, and enhanced vocabulary development.

Journal Writing

Having students respond to the quotes in writing, as either a lead-in or as an alternative to discussing the quotes as a class, addresses several language arts standards and serves as a terrific warm-up activity when your kids enter the room in the morning. To take advantage of this opportunity, simply write a quote on the board, along with one or more of the prompts listed below. You will quickly discover that certain prompts are more appropriate for some quotes than for others.

Give students approximately 10-20 minutes to write their responses. After providing a few moments for a pair-share, ask student volunteers to share their work with the whole group.

Journal Writing Prompts

1) Describe a time when you or someone you know demonstrated the main idea of this quote.

2) What do you think this quote means? Give examples.

3) Why do you think the speaker said this quote in the first place?

4) Do you agree or disagree with this quote? Explain why.

5) Describe how you can use the meaning of this quote to help you become a better student. Be specific.

6) Describe how you can use the meaning of this quote to help others.

7) Describe any word play or figurative language that you notice in this quote.

8) Describe both the literal and figurative meanings of this quote.

9) Describe how this quote can help you get along more effectively with other people.

10) Which habit(s) of character do you think this quote addresses? Explain why.

11) Do you see this quote connecting to your future in some way? If so, describe how.

Language Arts Standards

Discussing and writing about these character-building quotes addresses five of the twelve Standards for the English Language Arts established by the NCTE (National Council of Teachers of English) and IRA (International Reading Association). I list these standards below.

- Students apply a wide range of strategies to comprehend, interpret, evaluate, and appreciate texts. They draw on their prior experience, their interactions with other readers and writers, their knowledge of word meaning and of other texts, their word identification strategies, and their understanding of textual features (e.g., sound-letter correspondence, sentence structure, context, graphics).

- Students employ a wide range of strategies as they write and use different writing process elements appropriately to communicate with different audiences for a variety of purposes.

- Students apply knowledge of language structure, language conventions (e.g., spelling and punctuation), media techniques, figurative language, and genre to create, critique, and discuss print and non-print texts.

- Students participate as knowledgeable, reflective, creative, and critical members of a variety of literacy communities.

- Students use spoken, written, and visual language to accomplish their own purposes (e.g., for learning, enjoyment, persuasion, and the exchange of information).

Note About Gender

Should a quote refer only to "man" or "men," please emphasize that all quotes apply equally to members of both genders and that, most likely, the speaker lived during a time well before the women's rights movement began.

A Note About Song Lyrics

Some quotes are taken from song lyrics. Instead of having your child or student volunteers read these quotes aloud, play the lyrics on an ipod or other music player, with the device already cued to the spot in the song just before the quote, if possible. Hearing the quote sung by the original performer adds novelty, flair, and authenticity to the experience, gives greater meaning to the quote's message, and makes the activity more memorable for kids.

How This Book is Organized

Each of the following pages contains an inspirational quote and a corresponding set of "talking points" you may choose to use for reference when discussing the quotes with children.

Teachers, on the days you incorporate the quotes into your morning routine, you can glance at the talking points before your students arrive in class to prepare for the upcoming discussion.

Feel free to alter the sequence of the quotes should you wish to give greater or lesser emphasis to a particular habit of character or larger idea featured in the book.

Quote #1

"If you'll not settle for anything less than your best, you will be amazed at what you can accomplish in your lives."

-Vince Lombardi

* *

Pride

- A great quote to discuss at the beginning of a new school year. Discussing this quote helps establish a culture of high expectations and lets students know that their very best effort is expected every day.

- While this idea of maintaining the highest standard of effort may begin as a classroom expectation, the goal is for students to internalize it so that it eventually becomes a personal expectation.

Quote #2

"It is better to light a candle than to complain about the darkness."

- R. Herzog

* *

Positive Attitude

- This is another great quote to discuss at the beginning of a new school year. Discussing this quote helps your students develop a problem solving orientation and empowers students to take action when school's and life's inevitable challenges arise.

- Students are more likely to solve their own problems and less likely to complain or sit helplessly once this type of problem solving orientation is established in your classroom culture.

Quote 3

"Victories that are easy are cheap. Those only are worth having which come as the result of hard work."

-Henry Ward Beecher

* *

Perseverance

- Discussing this quote helps students understand that nothing worthwhile ever comes easily. Consistent hard work will be necessary to reach demanding goals.

- It's important for students to know that they won't be able to achieve many of their goals in a day or a week or a month; they will need to keep plugging away consistently, over time, to realize the results they are seeking.

- Sometimes working hard is interesting and exhilarating; sometimes it's not. Either way, we keep going with all our might.

Quote #4

"One hundred years from now, it will not matter what kind of car I drove, what kind of house I lived in, how much money I had in my bank account, or what my clothes looked like. But the world may be a little better because I cared enough to try to make a difference."

-Author unknown

* *

Service

- Discussing this quote can help students reflect on what's truly important in their lives. Of course, having money, shelter, and clothing is important, and if students want to make a lot of money and live in a big house, more power to them. Hopefully, though, they will also value service and try to make a difference in the lives of others.

- Take a minute to brainstorm with your students various types of service that they already perform or that they may wish to provide as they get older.

Quote #5

"The difference between ordinary and extraordinary is that little EXTRA!"

-Bonnie Hopper

* *

Self-discipline

- Some students may quickly recognize the word play involved with this quote and notice how by adding the word "extra" to the word "ordinary," the word "extraordinary" is formed.

- The message of this quote is another that we should strive to build into the culture of our classrooms early each school year: By consistently adding that little extra effort, putting in a little extra time, and caring a little bit more about our work, we can accomplish extraordinary things in the long run.

Quote #6

"Your body is a temple. Littering is strictly prohibited."

-Taken from the wall of a
Jamba Juice store

* *

Health/Wellness

- Taken from the wall of a Jamba Juice location, this quote is a metaphor that students should readily understand.

- Eating unhealthy foods is like littering our bodies. Just as we want to keep buildings clean, we want to keep our bodies clean by eating a variety of healthy foods.

- You can also discuss other ways people litter their bodies, such as smoking cigarettes, and the dangers associated with these ways.

Quote #7

"The game is never more important than the people you play it with."

-Pat Vickroy

* *

Kindness

· *Playing hard, competing, and wanting to win are legitimate parts of games and sports. This quote asserts, however, that the desire to win should never cause people to exhibit poor sportsmanship, cheat, or engage in behaviors that dishonor themselves or their fellow competitors.*

· *Our opponents are not our enemies, and our goal isn't to destroy them. Quite the opposite - we need our opponents, or else we wouldn't even have a game to play. Playing tug-of-war with nobody on the other side of the rope isn't very much fun.*

Quote #8

"Quality is the first thing you think about, the last thing you think about, and what you think about in between."

-Author unknown

* *

Quality

- My former teaching partner and I liked this quote so much that we had it on a wall for the entire year to emphasize the idea that in order to produce quality work, one must always keep that goal in mind, from the beginning of a project to the end.

- In addition, you can use this quote to highlight the difference between quality and quantity. Students need to know that what matters isn't how much they produce or how long their writing pieces are, it's how much care and quality they put into everything.

Quote #9

"The buck stops here."

- Harry S. Truman

* *

Responsibility

- This quote is all about taking responsibility for one's actions. When we make mistakes, we own up to them, try to correct them, and try to learn from them so we don't make the same ones again in the future.

- We view mistakes as teachable moments. The alternative is to deny responsibility, make excuses, and perhaps shift blame to others.

Quote #10

"If you do not think about the future, you cannot have one."

-John Galsworthy

* *

Success

- Young children have the ability to think about what they would like to do with their lives. Though the future can be a far-off, nebulous concept, students can express themselves well about such topics as the type of jobs they want and the academic areas they want to pursue as they get older.

- Ask a few volunteers to share some thoughts they have about the future. Without a doubt many will already be able to state the jobs they want and where they want to go to college.

Quote #11

"The greatest ability in business is to get along with others."

-John Hancock

* *

Cooperation

- A recent study found that the number one reason why people get fired from their jobs isn't that they don't know how to do their jobs well; it's that they don't work well and get along with their colleagues.

- Knowing how to cooperate with others is a necessary skill in business and a necessary skill in life. None of us lives on an island. In order for us to function productively in our schools, families, workplaces, and elsewhere, we need to value other people and make an effort to get along with them, especially those with whom we seemingly might not share much in common.

Quote #12

"If you can imagine it, you can achieve it. If you can dream it, you can become it."

-William Arthur Ward

* *

Courage

- *Discussing this quote can help children think beyond their current reality.*

- *Thinking big can motivate us to work harder and do what's necessary to make our dreams come true.*

- *It's important for students to know that dreams aren't wishes. Simply sitting back and wishing for things to happen won't, by itself, make it happen. Dreams must be coupled with hard work and dedication.*

Quote #13

"We are the music makers. We are the dreamers of dreams."

-Willie Wonka

* *

Positive Attitude

· This quote was Willie Wonka's response to Veruca Salt, who argued that there were no such things as snozberries.

· His point: if there's something that humans want to create, we have the imagination and determination necessary to do so, even if nobody else thinks such an undertaking is possible.

· Discussing this quote presents a wonderful opportunity to talk about well-known individuals, such as the founder of FedEx, who brought the world products, companies, and ideas that few others thought were doable.

Quote #14

"In every triumph there's a lot of try."

-Frank Tyger

* *

Perseverance

· Two aspects of this quote are worth highlighting with students.

· First, there's a bit of word play occurring, in that the initial three letters of the word "triumph" closely resemble the word "try."

· Second, in order for people to achieve any meaningful triumph or success, they must try their very best on a consistent basis.

Quote #15

"Derive happiness in oneself from a good day's work."

-Henri Matisse

* *

Pride

- An important message that teachers can model and deliver to students is that working hard feels good. Giving our best effort on a consistent basis instills pride, boosts our confidence, and makes us happy.

- In particular, discussing this quote can benefit students who tend not to be motivated on a consistent basis, as well as those who tend to be motivated primarily by grades or by pleasing others.

- The goal is for students to <u>want</u> to do great work because of the intrinsic joy and satisfaction found in the task, not feel that they <u>have</u> to do work.

Quote #16

"*Education can equip us to make a difference, and perhaps it can orient us toward making a positive one.*"

-Howard Gardner

* *

Service

- Students should be aware of the multiple reasons why attending school each day and working hard are important to their futures.

- A quality education can empower people to get the jobs they want, earn more money, earn admission to the colleges of their choice, maximize their options in life, reach other goals, and contribute meaningfully to society.

- This quote shines a spotlight on the final reason listed above: education provides the knowledge and skills people can use to help others.

Quote #17

"It's easier not to be great."

-From the song "I Alone"
by the group "Live"

* *

Self-discipline

- Though the meanings of many of these quotes may appear obvious to adults, they may not be as obvious to children. This quote serves as an example of this phenomenon.

- Kids need to know that it takes time, effort, and determination to achieve meaningful results in life. True greatness is rare and requires serious, uncommon commitment.

Quote #18

"It's the job that's never started that takes the longest to finish."

- J.R.R. Tolkien

* *

Patience

- Patience is one of the most difficult habits of character for young students to develop. Many times we procrastinate because a project appears daunting and overwhelming, and as a result, we never start it.

- Discussing this quote can help students take that first step. Once they do that, they can break longer endeavors into smaller, simpler parts and, hopefully, be more willing and better able to work patiently until the end.

Quote #19

"There is no exercise better for the heart than reaching down and lifting people up."

-John Andrew Holmes

* *

Kindness

- This quote addresses the word "heart" on two different levels, though the emphasis belongs mostly on the second.

- First, there's the physical aspect of exercise and how exercise strengthens the heart. You may want to ask your students to share some examples of physical activities that benefit the heart.

- Second, on an emotional level, giving people a boost, encouragement, and support (i.e., "lifting people up") helps them, of course, but it also makes us feel good.

Quote #20

"Be the change that you want to see in others."

-Gandhi

* *

Responsibility

- Setting a powerful living example is the most effective way to promote change in the world around us.

- Students who want others in the class to act more kindly, for example, would embody this quote by treating others with tremendous kindness, not by lecturing others, complaining about how unkind others may be, or throwing their hands up in despair.

Quote #21

"7 days without exercise makes one weak."

-Rudy Benton

* *

Health/Wellness

· Rudy Benton is a legendary Physical Education teacher from Northern California with a gift for clever word play.

· The key to this quote is the word "weak."

· Of course, seven days makes one week on the calendar. Seven days without exercise, however, makes one weak.

· Benton's point: keep your body healthy by moving it around on a regular basis.

Quote #22

"Success is not measured by what you do compared to others. Success is what you do compared to what you are capable of doing."

-Zig Ziglar

* *

Success

- It's natural for students to look around the classroom and wonder how they compare to other students with regard to reading, math, and other academic skills.

- Discussing the quote can help students understand that it really doesn't matter if anybody is better or worse than we are in any specific area; what matters is that we try our very best, maximize our unique potential, and perform as well as we are capable of performing.

- Trying to be better than everybody else is a losing battle. We should strive for personal bests.

Quote #23

"Rather fail with honor than succeed by fraud."

-Sophocles

* *

Honesty

· Students who work hard, behave honestly, and conduct themselves honorably can never be considered failures. Success will come, in time, to individuals who persevere.

· Students who lie, cheat, or seek short-cuts can never truly be considered successful - regardless of the results they achieve.

· How students earn their successes in life is just as important, if not more so, than the results they obtain.

Quote #24

"I am not afraid of storms, for I am learning how to sail my ship."

-Louisa May Alcott

* *

Courage

- Discussing this quote encourages children to consider how they view challenges. Do students view a challenging situation as something negative that they want to avoid or as something positive that they want to embrace?

- Part of building a quality classroom culture involves empowering children to develop a certain attitude, a certain mental toughness. Learning to see challenges as opportunities to test ourselves, dig deep, and bring out the best that's inside of us is an important part of that attitude.

Quote #25

"Bloom where you are planted."

-Proverb

* *

Positive Attitude

· We, as individuals, do not have the ability in life to choose where we are born, where we grow up, or who raises us. What we do have, however, is the ability to decide the kind of life we want to create for ourselves and the ability to decide that we will do everything in our power to make that dream a reality.

· Sadly, not every child is born into a happy, healthy situation, but every child needs to know that with enough hard work and dedication, the future can be significantly brighter than the past or present.

Quote #26

"Press on. Nothing in the world can take the place of persistence."

-Ray A. Kroc

* *

Perseverance

· This is a straightforward quote reminding us that when things don't go our way or when we run into obstacles, we have two choices. We can give up, or we can press on.

· Children also find it interesting to learn about Ray Kroc's background. After starting with one restaurant, he built his business into the largest restaurant chain in the world, McDonald's. It's interesting to discuss with students the kind of hard work and perseverance that must have taken.

Quote #27

"Every job is a self-portrait of the person who did it."

-Author unknown

* *

Pride

- *How our school work looks says a great deal about the type of students we are. Neat, careful, and organized work creates a favorable impression among those who read it, while sloppy, rushed, and careless work creates a far different impression.*

- *It's important to ask our students, "What does a typical piece of your work say about you?"*

- *Thinking about each piece of their school work as a self-portrait can have a powerful effect on young children and their motivation.*

Quote #28

"A candle loses nothing by lighting another candle."

-James Keller

* *

Service

- It's natural for children to watch a classmate receive a compliment and wonder, "What about me?" Students need to know that a kind word directed to somebody else is not meant as an insult directed at them.

- Rather than be competitive with others in this regard, we can understand that being kind, encouraging, and helpful to others makes all of us better and offers a win-win situation to everyone involved because it results in a warmer, friendlier environment where everyone feels appreciated and valued and where kind words are exchanged freely and easily.

Quote #29

"I found that the men and women who got to the top were those who did the jobs they had in hand, with everything they had of energy, enthusiasm and hard work."

-Harry S. Truman

* *

Self-discipline

- Individuals who are truly successful in their chosen fields aren't necessarily those who are the most intelligent and most talented; oftentimes, they simply wanted to succeed more than everybody else and were more determined.

- To help students understand this idea more completely, share some examples of well-known individuals who realized their dreams largely on the basis of hard work, such as Rudy Ruettiger, whose dedication earned him a spot on the Notre Dame football team and inspired a motion picture about his life.

Quote #30

"The reason we have two ears and one mouth is so that we may listen twice as much as we speak."

-Variation of a proverb

* *

Respect

- One of the best ways to learn and to show respect toward others is to listen closely to what they have to say.

- A note of caution: some children have the tendency to take this quote literally. So, we may need to point out that while we don't have to keep an exact count of how much time we spend talking and listening, we should always try to listen with an open mind and a genuine desire to consider other people's ideas, especially those opinions that may not match our own.

Quote #31

"The best vitamin for making friends: B1"

-Rudy Benton

* *

Kindness

· This is another clever quote from the aforementioned Rudy Benton.

· The central message of this quote: the best way to make a friend is to be a friend.

· Because many young children haven't yet learned the necessary skills for making and keeping friends, discussing these skills (e.g., giving compliments, using a kind tone of voice, displaying proper manners, doing favors, making and keeping promises, asking to play together, showing forgiveness) in conjunction with this quote can help students greatly.

Quote #32

"Those to whom much is given, much is expected."

- Variation of Norman Thomas quote

* *

Responsibility

- There are many people who believe that those who are blessed with exceptional skill, talent, or ability in a given area have a responsibility to develop that capacity to the greatest extent possible and use it to benefit others.

- We can extend this idea and discuss with our students how those of us who were fortunate enough to grow up with a loving family, shelter, food, and other necessities of life have a responsibility to their communities to try to provide help to those individuals who may not have been so fortunate.

Quote #33

"Do the work you love and love the work you do."

-Variation of David
Shakarian quote

* *

Health & Wellness

· A well-known expression states that if people are able to make a career out of doing what they love to do, they will never have to work a day in their lives.

· Some students may believe that a job is something they are supposed to get simply to earn a living; they may never have been exposed to the idea that a career can arise naturally from our passions and that there are ways to figure out how we can get paid to do what we love to do - and would do even if we weren't paid to do it.

Quote #34

"Failure is the condiment that gives success its flavor."

-Truman Capote

* *

Success

- *Just as condiments give flavor to and improve the taste of food, Capote suggests that failure improves the "taste" of success.*

- *When success doesn't come quickly or easily, we can either keep going with our efforts or we can quit. When we persevere and ultimately realize the success we seek, we appreciate it more and feel a greater sense of pride because we had to work harder to achieve it.*

- *This message about plugging away despite initial failure is one that students can't hear too many times.*

Quote #35

"Teamwork: many hands, many minds, one goal."

-*Author unknown*

* *

Cooperation

- *Many children are fortunate enough to participate in team sports or other group endeavors, such as an orchestra, that offer the joyous feeling of being a part of something greater than ourselves.*

- *Our classrooms can provide this same type of "team feeling." Discussing quotes such as this one reinforces the importance of working together, listening attentively, valuing the opinions of others, being unselfish, and other vital cooperative learning skills.*

Quote #36

"A man who wants to lead the orchestra must turn his back to the crowd."

-James Crook

* *

Courage

- Of course, this quote can be taken literally, but its figurative meaning is far more powerful and makes for a much more interesting discussion.

- Leaders have to do what is right or necessary, even if that decision is unpopular.

- Looking out for the best interest of the group isn't easy; it takes courage and integrity to stand up for what is right.

Quote #37

"Do what you can with what you have where you are."

-Theodore Roosevelt

* *

Positive Attitude

- This quote is similar to and reinforces the meaning of the earlier saying about blooming where you are planted.

- Rather than complain about having to live or work in less than ideal circumstances, we can make the best of the situation.

- Discussing this quote continues our efforts to build the optimistic, "can-do" spirit that lies at the core of a quality classroom.

Quote #38

"Nothing worthwhile ever happens quickly and easily. You achieve only as you are determined to achieve...and as you keep at it until you have achieved."

-Robert H. Lauer

* *

Perseverance

· This is another quote that emphasizes the value of patience, perseverance, and dedication.

· Because young children are inclined to seek immediate gratification for their efforts, we need to make a consistent effort to help our students develop a longer-term, future-oriented view of their progress. Discussing quotes such as this one is an important part of that effort.

· Ask your students to share examples of times in their lives when they showed persistence after encountering obstacles initially and ended up achieving meaningful goals.

Quote #39

"Whatever you are, be a good one."

-Abraham Lincoln

* *

Pride

- This is a terrific quote because it sets a high standard for all students to live up to, yet honors the uniqueness and individuality that all of us possess.

- The quote doesn't tell students what they should do with their lives; that choice is up to them. Lincoln simply states that they should give their all and take pride in what they do, whether it's as a doctor, lawyer, teacher, athlete, or something else.

Quote #40

"Ask not what your country can do for you, ask what you can do for your country."

- John F. Kennedy

* *

Service

- *In one of the most well-known quotes in American history, former President Kennedy highlights the importance of service.*

- *Instead of focusing on what others can do for us, Kennedy implores individuals to focus on what we can do to make our country a better place.*

- *For young children who tend to think primarily about their own needs, discussing the idea of service can help expand their perspective.*

Quote #41

"We are what we repeatedly do. Excellence, then, is not an act, but a habit."

-Aristotle

* *

Self-discipline

· It's important for students to understand that if they want to achieve excellence in their school work or in any other endeavor, they can't simply perform at a high level or put forth maximum effort one time or every once in a while. They must repeat this level of effort and performance consistently, over time, until doing so becomes a matter of habit.

· The word "act" in this quote means "one solitary act." Many children interpret the word to mean that a person is "pretending" to be excellent. Highlighting this difference may help children better understand the meaning of the quote.

Quote #42

"Quality = Caring"

-Robert Pirsig

* *

Quality

- When our goal is to produce quality work in school and elsewhere, the quote suggests that our attitude about the work we do is just as important as our knowledge and skills, if not more so.

- If we care enough about what we are doing and if we are willing to invest the necessary time, effort, and passion, we will eventually obtain quality results.

- Discussing this quote can be reassuring to dedicated students who often get nervous and worry about whether their best efforts will be good enough to get the job done.

Quote #43

"Peace begins with a smile."

-Mother Teresa

* *

Kindness

· Something as simple as a smile can produce powerful results, whether our goal is to try to make a new friend, settle an argument, diffuse a difficult situation, or lighten up a tense classroom environment.

· My students and I use the term "battery-chargers" to describe those individuals who brighten the mood and add positive energy to any room they enter.

· One characteristic that many battery-chargers share in common is that they are quick to smile and seem to be smiling all the time.

Quote #44

"Life is the acceptance of responsibilities or their evasion; it is a business of meeting obligations or avoiding them. To every man the choice is continually being offered."

-Ben Ames Williams

* *

Responsibility

- To maximize their unique potential, students must become the primary driving forces in their own education and their own lives.

- Rather than rely on help from their teachers and families, young people need to know that, every day, they own the choice of whether to accept their responsibilities. Once students make the decision to commit themselves fully to the cause of education, they become unstoppable.

- Taking responsibility for one's own learning is another core principle that we try to build into our classroom culture.

Quote #45

"*True enjoyment comes from activity of the mind and exercise of the body. The two are ever united.*"

-Humboldt

* *

Health & Wellness

·   Reminiscent of the ancient Greeks' emphasis on building a sound mind and a sound body, this quote helps students understand that in order to lead happy, balanced lives, we want to exercise our minds and exercise our bodies on a regular basis.

·   As part of this discussion, ask students to brainstorm a list of ways that people commonly do both of these things.

·   Also, be sure to discuss the quote's final sentence so students can see how exercising the mind benefits the body and exercising the body enriches the mind.

Quote #46

"There's no place where success comes before work, except in the dictionary."

-Donald M. Kimball

* *

Success

- Challenge your students to discover both the literal and figurative meanings of this quote.

- Literal meaning: the word "success" comes before the word "work" in the dictionary. (This presents a nice opportunity to review basic alphabetizing skills.)

- Figurative meaning: one cannot achieve success in any worthwhile endeavor without first putting in the necessary work. Said differently, success is impossible to obtain without hard work.

Quote #47

"No legacy is so rich as honesty."

-William Shakespeare

* *

Honesty

- When discussing this quote, it may be necessary at first to define the word "legacy" with your students.

- Consider asking your students to consider their own legacies. Specifically, ask them how they would like other people to remember them.

- Though others may remember them as able readers, creative writers, and great athletes, Shakespeare asserts that nothing is more important than being remembered as an honest person.

Quote #48

"The future belongs to those who believe in the beauty of their dreams."

-Eleanor Roosevelt

* *

Courage

- Even confident people have moments of self-doubt, and it's important for teachers to remind students frequently to believe in themselves and believe that they can make their dreams come true.

- Of course, obstacles will exist, but these obstacles can be overcome with passion, focus, hard work, enthusiasm, and determination.

Quote #49

"*For success, attitude is equally as important as ability.*"

-Harry F. Banks

* *

Positive Attitude

· This is one of many quotes in which the most powerful way to convey its message may be through the use of examples.

· With this quote I like to share the story of baseball player David Eckstein, who, despite being significantly smaller than most of his fellow competitors, exhibited tremendous determination and not only became a major league player, but helped the St. Louis Cardinals win the 2006 World Series, earning Most Valuable Player honors in the process.

Quote #50

"The successful man will profit from his mistake and try again in a different way."

-Dale Carnegie

* *

Perseverance

· *This is another quote that focuses on how people view mistakes. We can see them either as "bad things" that need to be avoided or as inevitable parts of life that offer valuable learning opportunities.*

· *It's important to emphasize to children that we all make mistakes, and we shouldn't be afraid to do so. Instead, we should learn from experience and try not to repeat our mistakes. In addition, if we're ever faced with a situation similar to one in which we erred the first time, we should approach things differently the next time and attempt a different strategy or plan of action.*

Quote #51

"To think only of the best, to work only for the best and to expect only the best."

- Taken from "The Optimist Creed"

* *

Pride

- We used the first quote in this book to help establish an environment of high expectations - of work, of effort, and of behavior. When discussing this quote, we can build on that foundation.

- Ask for student volunteers to share examples of how they or their classmates have brought the idea of high expectations to life in recent days and weeks.

- Specifically, you can pose the following question: "What are some ways in which you or your classmates have held high expectations for yourselves recently and then lived up to these expectations?"

Quote #52

"Man is not on the earth solely for his own happiness. He is there to realize great things for humanity."

-Vincent Van Gogh

* *

Service

- This quote is one of a few in this book that emphasizes the twin goals of doing great things for ourselves and doing great things for others.

- Finding the right balance can be difficult sometimes; many people tend to forego their own needs in trying to benefit others while it's also common to turn our focus inward and become so consumed with our own wants and needs that we neglect those around us.

Quote #53

"Doing the best at this moment puts you in the best place for the next moment."

-Oprah Winfrey

* *

Self-discipline

- Discussing this quote helps young students understand the cause-and-effect relationship that exists between the hard work we do now and the success we achieve in the long run.

- Though we may speak with our students a great deal about their futures, the only time over which we have control is the present. By taking full advantage of the time we have available in the present, the more we increase the likelihood that we will be successful in the future.

Quote #54

"The journey of a thousand miles begins with one step."

-Miyamoto Musashi

* *

Patience

- *When discussing this quote, we can review and extend the lessons of the earlier quote about procrastination and about how it can paralyze us into inaction when a job seems too overwhelming for us to handle.*

- *By taking that first step, though, we get ourselves off to a good start, build momentum and confidence, and shrink that large task into something a little bit more manageable.*

- *An active approach to problem solving always beats a passive one.*

Quote #55

"Friendship First,
Competition Second.

Winning or Losing is Only
Temporary

Friendship is Everlasting."

-Chinese Sporting Philosophy

* *

Kindness

- This is another quote that seeks to help children keep the concept of competition in proper perspective.

- By all means, play hard and try to win. At all times, however, remember that your opponents are people, too, not your enemies.

- We can be competitive and maintain our friendships at the same time. While the joy of winning and the disappointment of losing will soon fade, we hope to keep our friends around for a very long time.

Quote #56

"If we don't take action now, we'll settle for nothing later."

> *-From the song "Settle for Nothing" by the group "Rage Against the Machine"*

* *

Responsibility

- This quote emphasizes the importance of being proactive, taking charge, and going after what we want.

- Just sitting around hoping and wishing for great results will never bring about those results.

- This quote is another one that reminds students of the cause-and-effect link between consistent hard work and success.

Quote #57

"*Every child has inside him an aching void for excitement and if we don't fill it with something which is exciting and interesting and good for him, he will fill it with something which is exciting and interesting and which isn't good for him.*"

-Theodore Roosevelt

* *

Health & Wellness

- A significant part of our role in the classroom involves helping students find their passions, whether they involve sports, music, acting, writing, science, video games, or something else.

- Students who are aware of their passions have something to say "yes" to in their lives and, thus, will have an easier time saying "no" to the dangerous temptations they may encounter as they get older.

- Without these passions, students may believe that experimenting with cigarettes, alcohol, or other drugs is a good idea.

Quote #58

"The real moment of success is not the moment apparent to the crowd."

-George Bernard Shaw

* *

Success

- When Romanian gymnast Nadia Comaneci captured the world's attention with her gold medal performances in the 1976 Montreal Olympics, it was natural to think that her moment of success occurred with the eyes of the world upon her.

- In this quote Shaw is saying that her real moment of success happened well before that - behind the scenes when nobody was watching. It happened during those long years of training that led up to her Olympic victories. Ask your students to provide other examples of recent, successful performers who had to work long and hard before achieving their public successes.

Quote #59

"Quality cannot be obtained and improvement is impossible without cooperation."

-Rafael Aguayo

* *

Cooperation

- An increasing number of the world's jobs require people to work together, share ideas, and solve problems.

- To improve our work and obtain quality results, both in school and in our careers, we need to know how to cooperate.

- Without the ability and willingness to cooperate, our individual knowledge and skills will only take us so far.

Quote #60

"One who makes no mistakes never makes anything."

-Anonymous

* *

Courage

- *If we play it safe all the time and remain within our comfort zones, we may not make mistakes, but we're not going to grow either. We may not learn new skills, stretch ourselves in new directions, and increase our capacity for the future.*

- *Discussing this quote gives us another opportunity to help students develop a more positive view of mistakes, seeing them as valuable learning opportunities as opposed to seeing them as bad things that must be avoided.*

Quote #61

"Great hopes make great men."

-Thomas Fuller

* *

Positive Attitude

- In school we give a great deal of attention and recognition to our students for being great readers, writers, and scientists, but rarely do we discuss the concept of being a great dreamer or a great goal-setter.

- The higher we set the bar for ourselves, the more we are likely to accomplish.

- It's important to help our students think and dream big. Even though there will be inevitable setbacks and disappointments along the way, the results they obtain will be far greater than if they had expected less from themselves. High personal standards lead to great performance.

Quote #62

"When you reach the end of your rope, tie a knot in it and hang on."

-Thomas Jefferson

* *

Perseverance

· *Initially, students may need help understanding that the expression "reach the end of your rope" means that we have reached our frustration point.*

· *Instead of giving up when we encounter frustration or difficulty, Jefferson encourages us to hang on and keep going.*

· *This is another quote where we may want to challenge our students to identify both its literal and figurative meanings.*

Quote #63

"Go confidently in the direction of your dreams. Live the life you've imagined."

- Henry David Thoreau

* *

Pride

- *This is another of the quotes in this book encouraging our students to believe in themselves and feel confident in their ability to make their dreams come true - a message that cannot be repeated too many times.*

- *Ask for student volunteers to share one of the dreams they have for their lives and explain the type of hard work they will need to do to make it happen. For example, one student may share her desire to become an engineer and explain that she will need to do well in college and probably attend graduate school as well. Share some examples from your life.*

Quote #64

"Your life is worth more when you share it with others."

-Author unknown

* *

Service

- This is another of the book's quotes emphasizing the twin goals of doing great things for ourselves as well as doing great things for others.

- Taking time out of our days to help, spend time with, and bond with others enriches our lives, offers a win-win situation to everyone involved, and only makes our human experience more valuable and more worthwhile.

- When we give of our time and of ourselves, we gain a great deal more in return.

Quote #65

"Practice makes permanent."

-Norton Juster

* *

Self-discipline

- The more well-known expression *"Practice makes perfect"* is untrue because simply setting aside time to practice isn't enough.

- What matters is how you practice. Lazy, half-hearted practice will not lead to excellence; it will only lead to lazy, half-hearted performance - how you practice is how you will perform.

- Excellent practice leads to excellent performance.

- Discussing this quote can help students develop better, more diligent, more consistent study and work habits.

Quote #66

"Give so much time to the improvement of yourself that you have no time to criticize others."

- Taken from "The Optimist Creed"

* *

Respect

- Quality students are always working to improve themselves. These individuals reflect on their progress regularly, are aware of their strengths and weaknesses, and strive to build on those strengths and address those weaknesses on a consistent basis.

- When committing to this ongoing self-improvement effort, we know not to criticize others because it's disrespectful to do so and because we understand that we are all "works in progress."

Quote #67

"Man is so made, that whenever anything
fires his soul... impossibilities vanish."

-LaFontaine

* *

Success

- This quote highlights the power of motivation. The phrase "fires his soul" captures the idea of motivation in a way that is likely to resonate with students.

- When we are fully motivated to accomplish a task, there's almost no stopping us.

- Ask for student volunteers to share times in their lives when they accomplished something meaningful because they were so motivated (so fired up) to do so. Offer some examples from your own life.

Quote #68

"The price of greatness is responsibility."

-Winston S. Churchill

* *

Responsibility

- Discussing this quote helps students understand that if we want to be great at something, whether it involves school work, sports, or some other endeavor, we need to take full responsibility for ourselves.

- We need to make sure that we are the ones taking charge, setting goals, getting our work done, holding ourselves accountable, and maintaining high personal standards.

- It's wonderful if we are fortunate enough to have family, friends, and teachers to support us in our endeavors, but we can't rely on these people to do our work for us. The commitment must come from inside.

Quote #69

"Many people know how to work hard; many others know how to play well; but the rarest talent in the world is the ability to introduce elements of playfulness into work, and to put some constructive labor into our leisure."

-Sydney J. Harris

* *

Health & Wellness

- Many children learn early in life that hard work and having fun are mutually exclusive concepts. For example, they may hear comments such as, "OK, you've had your fun. Let's now get down to business."

- This quote expresses an alternative belief: that the two concepts are not mutually exclusive, but mutually enriching. Guided by this belief, when we make an effort to enjoy our work, our experience will be a more positive one, and our results will likely be better. The same idea holds true, according to Harris, when we add some labor into our leisure time.

Quote #70

"*Cooperate with knowledge and trust and you become invincible.*"

-Author unknown

* *

Cooperation

· In a group setting, when intelligent people share their knowledge, skill, and experience freely, and they are willing to listen to one another, value one another's input, and don't care who gets the credit, they will achieve astonishing results.

· When that degree of trust, openness, and unselfishness are not present, however, the group experience is likely to be far less productive and far less satisfying.

· The word "invincible" stands out to students and makes a powerful impression in terms of what they are able to achieve when they truly cooperate with others.

Quote #71

"Do the thing that is right even when the boss isn't looking because the boss isn't a criterion. The real boss is standing alongside you every moment of your life."

-Alfred P. Haake

* *

Honesty

- *This quote has the potential to launch a very interesting class discussion about why we behave the way we do.*

- *Do we behave one way when a boss or teacher or parent is watching us and a completely different way when nobody is watching us? Or, do we try to act in a way that we know is right, regardless of who is around?*

- *When students try to live up to their own high personal moral standards, regardless of whether anyone's watching, they show they understand that they are their own best boss.*

Quote #72

"Scratch your name into the fabric of this world before you go."

-From the song "Scratch Your Name" by the group "The Noisettes"

* *

Courage

- The phrase "Scratch your name into the fabric of this world" serves as an extremely clever, powerful call to action to students, encouraging them to make their mark in the world somehow.

- Ask students to share some ways in which they hope to make their mark in the world, both now and in the future. Their answers may be profound, such as trying to cure disease, but they don't need to be. Being a loyal friend, raising a terrific family, and helping to keep their neighborhoods clean are all fantastic responses.

Quote #73

"There are two ways of spreading light: to be the candle that sheds it or the mirror that reflects it."

- Edith Wharton

* *

Positive Attitude

- Battery-chargers who contribute ideas to the class, do favors for others, smile to ease a moment of tension, and spread their positive energy throughout the room perform an invaluable service to the group.

- In this quote Wharton is saying that others can make an equally important contribution to the group by extending, building on, sharing, and spreading these initial efforts; doing so multiplies their power.

Quote #74

"The habits of a vigorous mind are formed in contending with difficulties. Great necessities call out great virtues."

-Abigail Adams

* *

Perseverance

- Solving simple math problems or reading books well below our level does not strengthen our minds or challenge us to be at our best.

- We only learn and grow when we confront difficult challenges that force us to think, experiment with various strategies, and persevere.

- When students embrace difficult challenges, rather than try to avoid them, they will eventually develop a certain mental toughness that will serve them well throughout their lives, inside and outside of school.

Quote #75

"The rung of a ladder was never meant to rest upon, but only to hold a man's foot long enough to enable him to put the other somewhat higher."

-Thomas H. Huxley

* *

Pride

- The ladder metaphor in this quote can help students understand that in our 21st century world we can never become complacent.

- With the pace of technological change continuing to increase, we must continue to learn, grow, and improve our skills.

- Should we decide that our skills are already sufficient or "good enough," we run the risk of getting passed.

- None of us is already at such a high level in our chosen endeavor that we can afford to stop learning.

Quote #76

"Service is the rent we pay for the privilege of living on this earth."

-Marian Wright Edelman

* *

Service

- Edelman's quote is a strong one. It expresses the belief that service isn't something optional that people should do only if they have the time or the inclination; it's a responsibility that all individuals have in their lives.

- Ask your students about the type of service they currently perform at school, home, or elsewhere or the type of service they would like to perform in the future.

- You can also ask students to say whether or not they agree with the quote and to explain their reasoning.

Quote #77

"The first thing any man has to know is how to handle himself. Training counts. You can't win any game unless you are ready to win."

-Connie Mack

* *

Self-discipline

- This is another quote touching on the link between hard work and success.

- Beyond the "skill-building" aspect of preparation, former baseball manager Connie Mack also seems to be addressing the mental aspect of training, a component that includes building confidence and being mentally prepared to handle the game's (and life's) inevitable challenges.

- Ask students to try to apply Mack's quote about baseball to their lives in and out of the classroom.

Quote #78

"Quality is everyone's responsibility."

-Rafael Aguayo

* *

Quality

- *Traditionally, it has been the role of teachers to ensure that students produce quality work. When teachers assess progress, score papers, and assign grades, students naturally infer that their own role in ensuring quality is minimal or even nonexistent.*

- *Students need to understand that their role in ensuring quality is as important as the teacher's, if not more so.*

- *Asking students to self-evaluate their work, provide feedback to peers, and reflect frequently on their progress empowers them to fulfill this role well.*

Quote #79

"Show me the person you honor, for I know better by that the kind of person you are. For you show me what your idea of humanity is."

-Thomas Carlyle

* *

Respect

- Popular culture plays a huge role in the lives of young people, and it's natural for students to admire and emulate star athletes or the singers and actors of the day.

- Discussing this quote provides a wonderful opportunity to ask ourselves why we admire the people we do. Is it the fashion model who wears the latest clothes? Is it the basketball star who drives the most expensive car? Is it the parent who works two jobs to put food on the table? Is it the worker who stands up for the right of other workers to be paid a decent wage?

Quote #80

"The indispensable first step to getting the things that you want out of life is this: decide what you want."

-Ben Stein

* *

Responsibility

- Stephen Covey, well-known author of <u>The Seven Habits of Highly Effective People</u> and other books, shares the idea of "leaning your ladder against the wrong wall." When that happens, people spend their lives working hard to reach a certain goal, and when they reach it, they realize that it was the wrong goal.

- This quote helps all of us remember to spend time figuring out what it is that we really want out of life before beginning our climb up the ladder.

Quote #81

"I have learned that success is to be measured not so much by the position one has reached in life as by the obstacles he has overcome while trying to succeed."

-Booker T. Washington

* *

Success

- The world is full of individuals who overcame tremendous adversity to achieve the successes for which they are known today.

- These individuals can be found in all walks of life. They are musicians, politicians, writers, and athletes - just to name a few.

- We can use these success stories to inspire our students, especially the stories of individuals whose backgrounds most resemble their own and whose triumphs will be the most likely to resonate.

Quote #82

"I don't shine if you don't shine."

*- From the song "Read My Mind"
by the group "The Killers"*

* *

Cooperation

- *Discussing this lyric can help students understand the effect that each of us has on the others around us and on the classroom environment as a whole.*

- *While we certainly don't want our students to become dependent on others to make them happy, good feelings can be contagious, and if you're at your best, then that can help me be at my best.*

- *Some children make themselves feel better by putting other people down. The quote shows that the opposite situation is far more desirable - we make ourselves feel happy by making others feel happy.*

Quote #83

"All our dreams can come true if we have the courage to pursue them."

-Walt Disney

* *

Courage

- This quote is one of many in this book in which the speaker's central message can be brought to life effectively by discussing the speaker's life experiences.

- In this example you and your students can talk about who Walt Disney was, what his main accomplishments were, and how he might have needed courage to make his unique dreams come true.

- It's also wonderful if students have the opportunity to share their unique dreams and how they plan to pursue them, no matter what obstacles they encounter.

Quote #84

"What does not destroy me makes me stronger."

-Nietzsche

* *

Positive Attitude

- Other quotes in this book address the idea of learning from our mistakes, as well as the idea of viewing difficult challenges in a positive way, but this powerful quote takes these ideas to a new level.

- Believing that setbacks and hardships only make us stronger is a sign of incredible mental toughness and resilience.

- This type of attitude can serve us well during particularly trying moments and can often be the difference between success and failure.

Quote #85

"Big shots are little shots who kept shooting."

-Christopher Morley

* *

Perseverance

- This quote features a very clever example of word play, in that we don't often view a "big shot" as someone who does any actual shooting.

- Using this construct, though, helps us understand the quote's central meaning: we all have to start somewhere; none of us is born a "big shot." We become one by working hard, believing in ourselves, and never giving up.

- Some students, of course, may be unfamiliar with the term "big shot" and require a brief definition before discussing the larger meaning of the quote.

Quote #86

"Whether you think you can or you can't, you are right."

-Henry Ford

* *

Pride

- The way we perceive our ability to complete a task has a powerful effect on how we actually perform that task. If we think we will perform well at something, then we are likely to perform at our best. When we lack confidence, that doubt will usually manifest itself and interfere with our performance. A key aspect of this quote involves something called "self-talk," the messages we tell ourselves that can either lift or lower our spirits.

- Brainstorm and record with your students a list of "positive self-talk messages" they can use to encourage themselves during difficult tasks.

Quote #87

"A life is not important except in the impact it has on other lives."

-Jackie Robinson

* *

Service

- Similar to the Marian Wright Edelman quote about service being the rent we pay for the privilege of living on earth, Robinson's quote offers a powerful call to action.

- Brainstorming a list of ways that we can provide service to our friends and families is a great idea when discussing this quote.

- Charting your students' responses and following up on them in the days ahead only multiplies the positive effects of discussing this quote.

Quote #88

"Be just as enthusiastic about the success of others as you are about your own."

- Taken from "The Optimist Creed"

* *

Fairness

- Because it's so easy for young children to focus exclusively on their own needs and wants, discussing quotes such as this one can expand our students' perspective and help them see the bigger picture.

- Part of seeing the bigger picture involves understanding that as much as we enjoy feeling successful and receiving compliments, it's also important to acknowledge the success of others, give compliments freely, and be genuinely happy when others do a great job.

- Our classmates aren't our rivals, and their success doesn't indicate our failure.

Quote #89

"Long-range goals keep you from being frustrated by short-term failures."

-Anonymous

* *

Patience

· *Sometimes adults and kids can become so focused on the task at hand and caught up in the moment that we magnify our mistakes and blow them out of proportion.*

· *Because these situations happen rather frequently, it's important to help our students understand that progress toward our goals is rarely linear; more commonly, improvement is marked by peaks and valleys.*

· *Realizing that fact can help everyone remain calm and positive, despite occasional stumbles and frustrations.*

Quote #90

"There is a great man who makes every man feel small. But the really great man is the man who makes every man feel great."

-Chinese Proverb

* *

Kindness

- *This may be the ultimate quote to use in our quest to develop more battery-chargers in our classrooms.*

- *Battery-chargers have an unmistakable effect on those around them and provide a jolt of positive energy every time they enter a room.*

- *Consider brainstorming with your students a list of actions they can take to have more of a battery-charging effect on those around them.*

Quote #91

"All problems become smaller if you don't dodge them but confront them. Touch a thistle timidly, and it pricks you; grasp it boldly, and its spines crumble."

-William F. Halsey

* *

Responsibility

- Discussing this quote reinforces many of the characteristics we try to build into our classroom culture each year - being proactive, taking initiative, and solving problems independently.

- Use relevant examples from your classroom to bring this quote's meaning to life, ones pertaining to such issues as asking for help with homework, staying on track during long-term projects, and dealing with interpersonal conflicts.

- Procrastinating, blaming others, and ignoring issues in the hope that they simply go away aren't the answers.

Quote #92

"Be so strong that nothing can disturb your peace of mind."

- Taken from "The Optimist Creed"

* *

Health/Wellness

- This is another quote addressing the concept of mental toughness. Though developing this resilience in our students is an incredibly difficult task, it's definitely a worthwhile endeavor and an example of "leaning our ladder against the right wall."

- At any age it's difficult not to let a cruel comment or unkind word detract from our day, but when we reach the point when negative words directed our way don't shake our confidence or rattle our self-esteem, we have achieved something truly special that can last a lifetime.

Quote #93

"*Your success and happiness lie in you...Resolve to keep happy, and your joy and you shall form an invincible host against difficulties.*"

-Helen Keller

* *

Success

- *Regardless of what happens in the world around us, we all have the ability to choose how we want to feel and choose our mood.*

- *Though it's common to believe that the morning traffic caused us to be frustrated or that our cold coffee caused us to be cranky, it's more accurate to say that we chose to become irritated by these occurrences.*

- *Happiness is a choice, and we can discuss with our students how people are free to make this choice every day, no matter what difficulties we encounter.*

Quote #94

"*Courage is grace under pressure.*"

-Winston S. Churchill

* *

Courage

- Discuss with your students examples of individuals who were able to stay calm under extremely difficult circumstances and perform their responsibilities admirably.

- These examples can come from the world of politics, military life, sports, and many other fields.

- There's no reason why the individuals discussed need to be famous. Students may even be able to describe situations in which they, their family members, or their friends displayed grace under pressure.

Quote #95

"In the adult world it's the strength of your strengths, not the weakness of your weaknesses that really counts."

-Mel Levine

* *

Positive Attitude

- Schools operate with the noble intention of wanting, and expecting, all students to perform ably in every subject area.

- For those children who, despite their best efforts, experience serious difficulty in one or more of these areas, this quote can be extremely reassuring.

- Discussing this quote helps these children understand that when they get older, they will be able to chart their own course, one that emphasizes their areas of strength, capitalizes on their knowledge and skills, and caters to their interests and passions.

Quote #96

"I get knocked down, but I get up again. You're never going to keep me down."

-From the song "Tubthumping" by the group "Chumbawumba"

* *

Perseverance

· Many students will be familiar with the catchy song from which this quote comes.

· The lyric's rhythm, playfulness, and novelty offer us another terrific opportunity to reinforce the message that when life throws some adversity our way, we have two choices. We can either feel sorry for ourselves and quit or we can pick ourselves up, become more determined, and keep going.

Quote #97

"Believe you can change the world."

> -Carly Fiorina

* *

Pride

- This quote was the first of Hewlett-Packard's "Rules of the Garage" when Carly Fiorina was President and CEO.

- In addition to that rule, you may wish to share the entire set with your students.

  "Believe you can change the world.
  Know when to work alone and when to work together.
  No politics. No bureaucracy.
  The customer defines a job well done.
  Radical ideas are not bad ideas.
  Invent different ways of working.
  Believe that together we can do anything.
  INVENT!"

Quote #98

"The greatest honor history can bestow is that of peacemaker."

-Richard Nixon

* *

Service

- An earlier quote about honesty led to a discussion about how others will remember us, about our legacies.

- President Nixon's words extend this discussion and suggest that in addition to striving to be remembered for our honesty, we should conduct ourselves in a way that will cause others to remember us for our efforts to create more peace in the world.

- These efforts, of course, can range from the very small (a smile or a kind word) to the uncommonly large (leading a nation or civil rights group).

Quote #99

"*Keep your eye on the ball.*"

-*Proverb*

* *

Self-discipline

· Most students will immediately offer a literal interpretation of this quote, making connections to baseball and other sports where one needs to watch the ball in order to stay safe and be successful.

· While there's certainly nothing with discussing the literal meaning, greater attention should be given to the quote's deeper meaning - the importance of staying focused on our goals, avoiding distractions, and remembering what it is we're trying to accomplish so that we spend our time in the wisest possible ways.

Quote #100

"Seek first to understand, then to be understood."

-Stephen Covey

* *

Respect

· *One of Stephen Covey's well-known "Seven Habits of Highly Effective People," this quote presents the idea that we should care just as much about understanding the viewpoint of others as we do about wanting others to understand ours.*

· *Other people will be more likely to listen to our ideas when they know that we have listened carefully to theirs.*

· *While listening, we often tend to rehearse what we are going to say next instead of attending to the words, meaning, and emotion of what others are saying.*

Quote #101

"What lies ahead of you and what lies behind you are nothing compared to what lies within you."

-Mary Engelbreit

* *

Success

- Engelbreit's words are especially appropriate to discuss toward the end of the school year when one of our most important goals is to help students realize what they have accomplished during our time together. This is part of the valuable "cheerleader" role teachers can play.

- Spending several months talking about mental toughness, reinforcing this idea, and capitalizing on teachable moments pays off, and students should believe wholeheartedly in their ability to face difficult situations with confidence and strength.

Quote #102

"With great power comes great responsibility."

-Spiderman #7

* *

Responsibility

- This quote resembles an earlier one in the book and expresses the belief that those of us who are fortunate enough to possess great power in a given area have the responsibility to use that power for positive purposes and to develop that power to its full potential.

- Because children tend to associate the word "power" with physical strength or with being a boss or having control over other people, it's important to discuss other types of power, such as the power to write well, the power to persuade, and the power to lead others by example or by the strength of one's convictions.

Quote #103

"*Reading is to the mind what exercise is to the body.*"

-Richard Steele

* *

Health & Wellness

- Students will likely enter our classrooms with an understanding of how exercise can strengthen our muscles and help our bodies grow and develop, yet our kids may not understand that reading offers these same benefits to the mind.

- As part of this discussion, you may want to point out some of the specific benefits that reading offers: increasing our fluency, improving our comprehension, building up our vocabulary, lengthening our attention span, improving our spelling skills, and strengthening our imagination.

Quote #104

"*Each one of us, no matter what our task, must search for new and better methods - for even that which we now do well must be done better tomorrow.*"

-James F. Bell

* *

Quality

- One of the central tenets found in the literature about quality control and quality management is the idea of continuous improvement.

- Continuous improvement is an attitude more than it is a set of techniques.

- By helping our students develop a mindset where being complacent is never acceptable and where always striving to find ways to get a little better at everything we do is expected, we empower children to be successful in a rapidly-changing world that demands this type of improvement.

Quote #105

"The most important single ingredient in the formula of success is knowing how to get along with people."

-Theodore Roosevelt

* *

Cooperation

- When teachers discuss with students the idea of growing up to become successful in business and in life, we often focus on the academic skills required by many jobs, skills pertaining to reading, writing, math, science, technology, and other disciplines.

- As important as these academic skills, if not more important, are the social skills we all need to communicate effectively and work well with others.

- Displaying proper manners, accepting people for who they are, disagreeing without being disagreeable, and listening attentively are all critical for success.

Quote #106

"The ultimate measure of a man is not where he stands in moments of comfort and convenience, but where he stands at times of challenge and controversy."

-Martin Luther King, Jr.

* *

Courage

- *If you feel comfortable sharing some examples from your own life where you took a difficult stand or did something that you believed was right, even though it wasn't easy or popular, students will remember your words for a long time to come. Personal examples are powerful, and they will resonate loudly.*

- *Whether you do or don't choose to share, ask your students to share examples from their lives or from the lives of others. This type of discussion has the potential to build tremendous mutual respect among the kids in your class.*

Quote #107

"The longer I live, the more I realize the impact of attitude on life. Attitude, to me, is more important than the past, than education, than money, than circumstances, than failures, than success, than what other people think or say or do."

- Charles Swindoll

* *

Positive Attitude

- Many of the quotes in this book relate to having a positive attitude, developing a resilient mindset, and being a battery-charger.

- Swindoll's quote nicely ties these ideas together and powerfully expresses just what a significant factor having a positive attitude can be in our ultimate success and happiness.

- As part of this discussion, you may want to discuss related ideas, such as looking at the bright side of things, finding the good in difficult situations, and remaining determined even in the face of long odds.

Quote #108

"He who would learn to fly one day must first learn to stand and walk and run and climb and dance; one cannot fly into flying."

-Nietzche

* *

Perseverance

- A video game analogy works well when discussing the meaning of this quote.

- Kids know full well that they can't start a game at level one and instantly advance to the highest level. Such progress takes time, experience, patience, and incremental successes.

- This same idea of step-by-step improvement holds true for our academic work, as well other endeavors that children value, such as sports, music, and other performing arts.

Quote #109

"Go big or go home."

-Del Taco Commercial

* *

Pride

- In recent years this quote has gained great popularity and has been referenced in a wide variety of movies, television shows, and commercials.

- Though the quote is often used in a lighthearted, even comedic, context, its message is a powerful one: if you're going to do something, do it with all your might.

- Half-hearted effort or performance is never acceptable and will rarely lead to success.

Quote #110

"*The true measure of a man is not the number of servants he has, but the number of people he serves.*"

-Arnold Glasgow

* *

Service

- Our society tends to define success in terms of financial success. For example, when someone describes an attorney as being successful, we can typically infer that the attorney earns a significant amount of money.

- This clever quote turns that idea on its head. When discussing success, it's not about the amount of wealth that person possesses, it's about the amount of service that person provides.

- Viewing success in terms of what one gives instead of what one possesses is illuminating and opens up many potentially interesting avenues of conversation.

Quote #111

"With Live, it's Game 7 every single night."

- From the song "Transmit Your Love" by the group "Live"

* *

Self-discipline

· In professional sports such as baseball and basketball, championships are decided in a best-of-seven series where the first team to win four games is crowned the champion. When a series is tied three games apiece, Game 7 is the deciding game and is, thus, the game where the teams' focus and intensity reach their highest levels.

· In this lyric the band "Live" makes the point that they bring their best focus and intensity to the concert stage every night.

· In short, the message to kids is that they should always put forth maximum effort.

Quote #112

"Quality means a demanding, difficult, never-ending effort to improve."

-*Lloyd Dobyns & Clare Crawford-Mason*

* *

Quality

- This straight-forward quote describes exactly what it means for an individual or a group to embrace quality as a top priority.

- Pursuing quality is a journey with no endpoint. Even when things are going well and we feel highly successful in our chosen endeavors, we understand that we must keep getting better, no matter how difficult or demanding that improvement effort becomes.

- The world around isn't slowing down; neither can we.

Quote #113

"If you have not often felt the joy of doing a kind act, you have neglected much, and most of all yourself."

-A. Nielsen

* *

Kindness

· It's critical for young children to understand that kindness doesn't simply benefit the recipient of a kind word or act, but the giver as well.

· When we show kindness toward others, of course they will feel better, but so will we.

· Being kind offers a win-win situation to everyone involved.

· Discuss with your students the idea of "a random act of kindness" and encourage them to commit these acts frequently for their families, their friends, and, most important, their teachers.

Quote #114

"I've always been in the right place at the right time. Of course, I steered myself there."

-Bob Hope

* *

Responsibility

- Many times individuals attribute their success to chance, luck, or good fortune.

- While these factors may play a role in our success to an extent, our hard work, planning, preparation, and good judgment almost always play a much larger role.

- If we rely on luck or chance, then we relinquish control of our fate to outside forces. By working hard and doing everything in our power to put ourselves in a position to be successful, we rely on ourselves, and we acknowledge that we are in control of our fate.

Quote #115

"*Literacy is a form of power...power to affect or transform that world.*"

-*Nelda Cambron-McCabe &*
Janis Dutton

* *

Health & Wellness

- From a young age, children hear from parents and teachers about the importance of literacy skills, most notably reading.

- So that students don't view literacy as simply a "school thing," it's crucial that children understand the larger role that reading, writing, speaking, and listening skills play in evaluating information critically, influencing people's opinions, persuading us to do and buy certain things, and shaping the world around us.

- Discussing this quote is especially relevant these days due to the explosion of communication tools now available.

Quote #116

"The world is moved not only by the mighty shoves of the heroes, but also by the aggregate of the tiny pushes of each honest worker."

-Frank C. Ross

* *

Honesty

- Though the actions of well-known, powerful individuals, such as presidents and kings and generals, tend to capture the headlines, everyone has a role to play in making the world a better place.

- We all have the ability and the power to contribute to the lives of our families, friends, and communities.

- Just because some people don't earn tremendous sums of money, possess a powerful title, or gain attention from the media, that doesn't mean their efforts to improve the world are any less important than those of others who are more famous.

Quote #117

"*Little drops of water wear down big stones.*"

-*Anonymous*

* *

Perseverance

· *Just as drops of water can eventually wear down big stones, consistent hard work, perseverance, and determination can eventually help us solve seemingly insurmountable challenges, complete large-scale projects, and reach long-term goals.*

· *The key is not to become overwhelmed by intimidating endeavors and simply get started. Once we take the first step, the remaining ones usually seem smaller and more doable.*

· *There's no reason to procrastinate or feel powerless in the face of a big challenge.*

Quote #118

"You can influence the future only by what you do today."

-John Wooden

* *

Success

· One could fill an entire book of quotes with pearls of wisdom from John Wooden, UCLA's legendary basketball coach who passed away in 2010 and whose books and "Pyramid of Success" are worthy of further exploration with your students.

· This quote reminds us that even though we may emphasize the importance of the future in our classes, we will never spend one minute there. We only have control of the present, and by taking full advantage of our opportunities in the present, we maximize our options for the future.

Quote #119

"Success comes in cans, not cannots."

-Joel Weldon

* *

Positive Attitude

- Children enjoy discussing the clever word play this quote features, and our literal thinkers may need to be reminded that true success doesn't come in actual cans.

- Adopting a "can-do" attitude helps us become more successful. In other words, figure out a way to get the job done rather than complain about how difficult a task may be or may appear to be before starting it.

- We will be more successful when we focus on what we are able to do rather than what we may not yet be able to do.

Quote #120

"If you are grinning, you are winning."

-Author unknown

* *

Health & Wellness

- Caring deeply about our work and being determined to succeed doesn't mean that we need to have sour, intense looks on our faces all day long.

- Working hard and having fun are mutually enriching concepts, not mutually exclusive ones. Producing quality work should be enjoyable and feel good.

- Enthusiastic learners who enjoy themselves as they go about their business and keep a smile on their faces usually produce better work than others who take themselves too seriously and aren't having any fun.

Quote #121

"You are the artist.
Your life is the canvas.
Your deeds are the paints.
You are creating a masterpiece."

-Norm Homie

* *

Quality

- A beautiful, inspirational quote to save for the last day of the school year, Homie's words help all of us take a step back and reflect on the wonderful growth achieved during the preceding months.

- Sometimes we (both teachers and students) are so focused on addressing weaknesses and turning them into strengths that we forget about all the triumphs we have achieved, all the progress we have made, and all the quality we have produced.

- It's important to understand that in our own unique way, each of us is, indeed, working hard to create a masterpiece.

Made in the USA
San Bernardino, CA
16 October 2017